NO. 17

UNIVERSITY OF MINNESOTA PAMPHLETS
ON AMERICAN WRITERS   65 CENTS

E. A. Robinson

BY LOUIS COXE

PAMPHLETS ON AMERICAN WRITERS · NUMBER 17

UNIVERSITY OF MINNESOTA

Edwin Arlington Robinson

BY LOUIS COXE

UNIVERSITY OF MINNESOTA PRESS · MINNEAPOLIS

Printed in the United States of America at the
Lund Press, Inc., Minneapolis

Library of Congress Catalog Card Number: 62-62785

Excerpts from *Collected Poems of Edwin Arlington Robinson* (1937)
are quoted by permission of The Macmillan Company.

PUBLISHED IN GREAT BRITAIN, INDIA, AND PAKISTAN BY THE OXFORD
UNIVERSITY PRESS, LONDON, BOMBAY, AND KARACHI, AND IN
CANADA BY THOMAS ALLEN, LTD., TORONTO

EDWIN ARLINGTON ROBINSON

⌐ Edwin Arlington Robinson

GRANTED a real talent and an access to experience, a poet deserves the name and earns it chiefly by his honesty. It is never enough that he be up with or beyond the times; who knows what those are? Technical feats rise, shine, evaporate, and fall, and there are unread poets who could have taught Shakespeare lessons in prosody. The sources from which poets "steal" metaphors and ideas often show the difference between knowing all about poetry and being a poet: it is not a matter of know-how, for if it were, Abraham Cowley would be greater than John Milton and Edward Young than Samuel Johnson. What is necessary is to see and to say with that direct honesty of vision that is apparently accessible only to genius and is therefore to the ordinary critic the least readily detectable of poetic qualities. A passion torn to tatters, a fit of the vapors, or a commitment to slogans of whatever degree of sophistication does not argue a true poetic vision; what counts supremely is the double commitment to the Muse and to the view of things the Muse inspires. In many cases, poets take years to find the vision, to see it for what it is, and that seeing may be only momentary and fleeting, but we know ultimately whether the poet has seen indeed or whether he has merely faked and trumped up. Larger or smaller, deeper or shallower, vision truly seen and honestly shown marks the poet, and it may be said fairly enough that in few instances have the contemporary critics shared enough of the visionary power or the honesty to see the poet's for what they are.

Edwin Arlington Robinson is a poet of true vision and unimpeachable honesty. Lest that sound forbidding — suggestive of something crabbed, angular, and inept — one should add that he had a consummate mastery of versification and rhetoric, that he could pile on the colors with the best of them, and that he had the inventiveness to tease the mind with symbol and intellectual puzzle. He indulged these capacities from time to time, the latter most frequently, but not until his later years did he allow them to assume the upper hand. All of Robinson's best work is the product of a sensibility that was on guard against fraud, that concerned itself with making into form what vision had discovered. The word "seeing" occurs frequently in Robinson, on various levels of seriousness and relevance; for this poet honesty is not so much what one has as what one tries to achieve after however much time spent among deceptions, lies, illusions. He knew a great many people, including members of his own family, who perished by such chimeras. He was born into, and grew to full maturity in, a time that is a kind of *locus classicus* for all lies on whatever scale. See Henry Adams, the later works of Mark Twain, and any history of the years just before the Great War and of that war itself. The era marked Robinson, for good and for ill. It disillusioned him with democracy and with the classic New England liberalism, and it "dated" him hopelessly in the eyes of the later generation of poets and literary folk.

To an older friend he wrote from his deathbed in the New York Hospital: "I doubt if you would care much for Auden and Spender. They are for the youngsters." It is not untypical of the man that he should have read these poets and be in a position to speak of them, yet give the impression of being the old fogy; ironically he puts himself in the position of his correspondent, who was twenty years his senior, and sees perfectly the faults of that rigidity of taste and habit likely to come with age. The diffidence, the hesitancy, with which he always expressed and qualified opinions stayed with him all his life, even in the era of his apparent pre-eminence after achiev-

6

ing both fame and something like fortune. His fine poem "Hill-crest," written at the artists' summer colony in Peterborough, New Hampshire, which was founded and maintained by the widow of the musician Edward MacDowell, expresses his acute sense of the insignificance of human achievement and the ephemeral nature of any one man's claim to rightness. He was a considerable "lion" at the MacDowell Colony during his latter years and he enjoyed being lionized, yet he never forgot that ". . . great oaks return / To acorns out of which they grew." In 1925, with a Pulitzer prize and other awards to his credit (if that is the phrase!), he wrote thus to a friend asking for a *Blue Guide* to London: "I'm not going to London, but sometimes I like to take up that book. It is almost as exciting as an illustrated seed catalogue, and far more reliable. . . ."

Small wonder that the generation of Pound and Eliot did not find Robinson's work and aesthetic congenial, chiefly because they never took the trouble to read him, but also, and understandably, because the era of which Robinson was inevitably part had finally ended in the hitherto unknown destructiveness of World War I. The period between the American Civil War and the War to end War may seem to us in retrospect not to lack appeal; to those who lived in it, like Henry Adams and Mark Twain, it seemed the shabbiest, most degrading of times. We can read their separate records of it: *The Education of Henry Adams* and *The Gilded Age*; in the latter, Twain created the most memorable of all fictional persons representative of the promoter in that raucous era, Colonel Beriah Sellers, the immortal speculator and harebrained proponent of get-rich-quick. He might well have been the spiritual godfather of Robinson and of his entire generation.

Robinson's youth and young manhood, the years leading up to *The Torrent and the Night Before* (1896), seem to have been lived in a barren time indeed. He was born in the tiny village of Head Tide, Maine, in 1869, at the very dawn of the Gilded Age, and

7

though the family moved very shortly thereafter to the larger town of Gardiner, Maine, on the Kennebec River, we today can see both the provinciality on the one hand and the national craze for speculation and wealth on the other which equally marked the Robinson family and many others of the period. Despite all that might be said of Maine's natural beauty, its classical New England heritage, its abiding interest in learning and literature, and its tough moral legacy of Puritanism (rather less severe in Maine than elsewhere in New England), the fact remains that the Gardiner of 1870–1900 was a typical American boom town with its trade in lumber, ice, and shipping as well as certain manufactures. The more substantial capitalists of the town had interests in western properties and speculative enterprises: lumber, land, railroads, mines. And just as the depredation of the land of Maine and other parts of the country typified the attitude of the exploiters, so did their driving, piratical Philistinism in the arts and culture generally set the tone of public and private taste. Poetry, real poetry, had to go underground. From the death of Emily Dickinson (and who had ever heard of her?) in 1886, and of Whitman in 1892, until the renascence at the time of World War I, there is almost literally nothing in the poetry of America. Stephen Crane died young and inchoate; all the early promise of Vachel Lindsay and Edgar Lee Masters turned to little or nothing much, and the one truly impressive, salient figure of this lonely time is that of the lonely, dedicated, self-deprecating man for whom, if ever for any poet, the time was out of joint.

Robinson's father had moved to Gardiner in anticipation of a boom in his business; he was concerned in the lumber trade and had ventured into speculation in western property. He was a man of a not insensitive nature and in different circumstances might have shown his oldest and youngest boys more sympathy. The poet's mother was a woman of some literary taste, though perhaps we may feel free to be skeptical of the quality of such taste as it impinged upon the sensibility of her son. It should be said that in Robinson's early years he read as poets usually do: widely, omnivorously, wholly without discrimination, and it may be that much that was bad had as strong an effect upon him as the good. Be that as it may, the good was not entirely lacking, in literature, education, and recreation. There was a literary set in Gardiner and notable among its members was Dr. Alanson Tucker Schumann, a physician and poet whose infatuation with poetry led him to Robinson when the latter was a boy in high school. Perhaps Robinson may have had him partly in mind when he spoke in "The Wandering Jew" of a "fealty that presents / The tribute of a tempered ear / To an untempered eloquence." But the boy learned a great deal from Schumann, particularly verse forms and a respect for them. Under that kindly tutelage Robinson wrote ballades, villanelles, rondeaus, and other forms so dear to the post-Pre-Raphaelite heart. Nor was the regimen anything but beneficial: Schumann was a taskmaster and Robinson learned a respect for scrupulous workmanship the results of which may be seen not only all through his work, but more directly in such early poems as the villanelle "The House on the Hill," which exhibits the typically Robinsonian merging of the old, traditional form with the laconic, sinewy plain diction that was both new and typical of the region, and "The Ballade of Broken Flutes," Robinson's statement of his mission as the bringer of a new kind of poetry. Is it mere coincidence that the poet's mother was descended from the family of America's first poet, Ann Bradstreet?

And of course Gardiner was the home of Laura E. Richards, the daughter of Julia Ward Howe who wrote "The Battle Hymn of the Republic." Mrs. Richards was an author and the friend of authors; whatever one may think of her taste and her own literary work, one must acknowledge both her great humanity and her insight. She practically dragged the young, shy poet out of hiding and into her ebullient, charming family where Robinson found another home after his own had disintegrated. Here he found stimulation of various kinds: the companionship of Mrs. Richards, her architect husband, and their sons and daughters, and simple recognition as a poet. True, we may see in the influence of the family certain limiting factors, of taste and of ideas, but Mrs. Richards was certainly on sure ground in preferring and encouraging the lyrical rather than the philosophical Robinson. It would seem that Robinson himself took little advice from anyone throughout his career, but he took from the Richardses affection and a sense of identity as poet. Perhaps Miss Rosalind Richards is the woman of Hagedorn's hints (in his biography) and perhaps we shall know one day when the documents pertaining to the poet deposited in the Houghton Library at Harvard are made available.

Love and marriage were not to be for Robinson. Gardiner, the Tilbury Town of the poems, left a mark on him, in part because of its very nature as a town of its time and place and in part because of the personal tragedies and wounds he knew there. So many of the portraits of his early volumes seem drawn from the life, his own or another's, that the reader never forgets what Gardiner meant to him always. For years the young man was to all intents and purposes an idler and a failure; the consciousness that he was so considered embittered him far beyond anything the actual opinion of his fellow townsmen seems to have warranted. Many admired and liked him, but it was not a merely parochial matter with Robinson: his response to the realization that he was indeed a poet is characteristically American. If art is considered trivial and idle in America, he might have said, then I can justify my life and work only by success. And success means publication and profits, money and position. After all, Gardiner, along with all America, strove mightily with Roscoe Conkling, the Stalwart Republican from New York, and President U. S. Grant for the power and the money that are success, and when in their turn Robinson's father and both brothers failed in the scramble, the young man might well have felt in his heart that he was doomed with the rest of his kin. He saw, in any event, a vision of American life that marked him permanently. The moral collapse of his brothers, on top of the horrible death by diphtheria of his mother and the disintegration of his father, could scarcely be accounted for by the philosophies and theologies of a century of New England storekeepers. After all, Puritanism no longer worked as a creed; Unitarianism had given way to Mrs. Eddy's gospel of Christian Science, and the sages of Concord provided pretty thin gruel to the hungry poet of the Grant-McKinley dispensation.

The young Robinson, classically, was a sensitive youth — he was born with his skin inside out as he said himself — and though he had friends (friends were his passion) and loved his years at the Gardiner High School, he was always an enigma to his associates and to his family, who let him go his dreamy way, but scarcely thought that he would ever outshine the brilliant, handsome Dean, the oldest, or the driving, vital Herman, next in order. To a Freudian, all things are Oedipal and there is indeed a case for seeing in Robinson's life the familiar pattern of the unwanted third son, rejected, kindly enough, by the father and kept at a distance by a too-beloved mother. In his later years, Robinson seems to have gained help from a psychiatrist who was also a poet, Dr. Merrill Moore. Gardiner in the eighties and nineties knew no such amenities, and one may perhaps be permitted to feel a callous relief since if Robinson had the anguish, we have the poetry. Yet we must feel pity as well, for the years following Robinson's graduation from high school, with the exception of two at Harvard, must have been an almost unrelieved agony of soul. Dean, the star of the family, was breaking up under the influence of drugs; he contracted the habit while trying to force himself into the exhausting routine of a country doctor. The father, Edward Robinson, decayed physically while his investments vanished; Herman, now married and with two small daughters, somehow seemed to have lost his way. Colonel Beriah Sellers like a proper godfather had vowed things in Herman's name. Yet before the smash became total, E. A. R. had his two years as a special student at Harvard. Following a period of isolation and near-despair after his graduation from high school, Cambridge, Boston, and Harvard came as deliverers and saviors. The young poet learned something of languages and literatures, of taverns and aesthetics, of the theater and above all of opera, particularly Wagner. When the money gave out and he had to leave, he even then knew he had been saved, though Barrett Wendell, the critic and Harvard professor, years later, when Robinson told him he had to leave Harvard after two years, growled, "You were damn lucky." Perhaps he was.

Try as one will, one cannot help the conviction that throughout his life Robinson was the victim of the classic strategy of America with its artists, poets in particular, perhaps. It would seem that the formative years provide a diet too thin, too miserly and deficient in nutriment, the last years a regimen of indigestible fats: success, when and if it comes, comes with a vengeance, frequently confirming the artist in his worst faults and conferring on him both an authority of opinion beyond his competence and opportunities to sell not just his work but himself to commercial interests. But before Robinson could have reached any such position, he knew fully what neglect and unsuccess could be. His was for a time the world of the down-and-out, the panhandlers and outcasts. Abject poverty and slavery to alcohol went hand in hand. In later years he himself said that the only thing that saved him was that he never took a drink before six in the evening.

Yet the worst was isolation, isolation from the best minds of his time and from those whose work and thought might have been useful and encouraging to him. Kind, understanding, and helpful as Robinson's friends were (and indeed they kept him alive and in health for years with simple charity), they do not seem to us today men and women who could have helped him in his struggle to learn and to grow as a poet; in all humility, we must call them second rate. Of the poets with whom he was well acquainted, three names stand out: William Vaughn Moody, Josephine Preston Peabody, and Ridgely Torrence, of whom the first two were far better known in their time than Robinson. There were literary figures of various shades of distinction among his friends and associates, notably Mrs. Richards, yet again there was none who seemed to have the insight into the true quality of his best work that would have helped the poet to grow. For all the voluminous correspondence with the literary and near literary which carried Robinson on through many years, there can be no escaping the conclusion that time, place, and circumstance conspired to deprive him of incentives toward development, growth, and change. His first book sets a pattern which will not be broken, and in his beginning is his end.

Robinson is a nineteenth-century product, a Romantic, and a scion of the New England stock. Did he not say himself that had he lived in the time of Brook Farm he would have been strongly tempted to go along? One can see in him the qualities that made a Jones Very, and although he repudiated both Thoreau and Emerson, as philosophers or thinkers, he admired Emerson's poetry, saturated himself in nineteenth-century prose and poetry, and generally conformed to the canons of taste of the sensitive, provincial, cultivated New Englander. It was some old atavistic urge that led him to Poe and to Hawthorne, to the darker side. He seems to have known nothing of Melville, though he liked Whitman and Twain, particularly the former, but it should be said that like most New Englanders of the age, his eyes were on England rather than his own country — for literature at least — and surely his love of Cowper and Crabbe shows how much more comfortable he was with traditional English verse than with that of the Decadents. He dismissed the *Yellow Book* as mere sensation. He seemed to feel kinship among poets of the nineties only with Kipling and Hardy. And all his tastes, like his ideas and convictions, came early and came to stay. In this as in so much else he is typical of his race and milieu, the New England eccentric with the eccentricity raised to genius and the right to his crotchets confirmed and made great by virtue of his earning and living that right to the end and with the utmost rigor. It is not too much to say that Robinson worked out to its conclusion and at large what Emily Dickinson, tentatively, found and named in the decay of the New England sensibility. The tradition still lives, and strongly, in the work of Robert Lowell, in whose dramatic soliloquies or monologues one may find the plain, vital influence of Robinson and his peculiar, involute syntax. *The Mills of the Kavanaughs* is Lowell's obeisance – and perhaps farewell – to his master.

After the destruction of family ties, for the most part, with Gardiner, Robinson went to live in New York, where he stayed almost without intermission, except for long summers at the MacDowell Colony, until his death in 1935. He knew poverty so great that he was often without proper food and clothing and lived on the charity of his friends. His first books made no impression on the "little sonnet men" who reviewed for magazines, nor did any periodicals think it worth while to publish this unknown when after all Clinton Scollard and George Edward Woodberry and many another sweet-singer were the acknowledged masters. Robinson's first two books were published at his own expense and that of friends, and the manuscript of *Captain Craig* (1902) languished in a brothel until the editor who had left it there came back, not presumably for the manuscript. He turned it down in any case. In 1905, President Theodore Roosevelt, who had heard of Robinson's work through his son Kermit, found a place, a sinecure, in the New York Custom House for the poet, and for four years Robinson knew financial independence. He also knew bondage to drink. At any rate, he did not write much in these years at the Custom House; it was an extended period of

14

frustration which finally disappeared, and in 1910 he published *The Town Down the River.*

In this volume we may see the typically Robinsonian themes and approaches, but with possibly three exceptions, none of the poems represents the finest he could do. "For a Dead Lady" surely shows him at his best in one of his veins, and to a lesser extent and in a less formidable vein, "Two Gardens in Linndale." And "Momus" has a terse, bitter strength that characterizes the epigrammatic strain that is one of his most pungent. It would appear that in these years Robinson was looking for a stance, a position from which to view his own experience and his ideas. As he grew older and took to writing the long narrative poems, his tendency to become oracular, cryptic, and philosophical by turns overcame the achieved starkness of his view; moreover in his letters one may find evidence that Robinson, when he was at his best as poet, had no thoroughgoing idea of his own best qualities. At one time a young lady who was writing a graduate thesis on the philosophy in his work wrote to ask him certain questions. In his reply he told her that he wished she would concern herself less with the philosophy and more with the poetry, a recommendation we may properly wish the poet himself had adopted. For the fatal New England fascination with cloudy abstractions miscalled thought or profundity overcame Robinson and he never broke the spell, except as it would seem almost inadvertently. Even in as interesting a long narrative as *Amaranth* (1934) the nightmare atmosphere, the very real subject, the grim humor, and the subdued lyricism frequently get lost in the interminable rehashing of Favorite Transcendentalisms: what is Truth? or Reality? In the Arthurian trilogy of a few years before we can see much the same tendency.

Robinson is a late Romantic, a Victorian, a Transcendentalist whose lust after the abstract was inveterate and nearly always, when indulged, destructive. The moment of stasis, of balance, when he treats the Vast with steady eye and nerve, is to be found in "The Man against the Sky" in the volume of that title (1916); he met the subject with all its imponderables and impalpables head on in that poem, and never fully recovered. Although "The Man against the Sky" solves nothing — and it is of course unfashionable to do other than dismiss it — it nonetheless seems to be almost the last time in literature (Western) when a poet singlehanded calls down the Eternal Verities and Cosmic Powers and asks them to declare themselves. It is an altogether remarkable performance and would have been wholly impossible for a more "sophisticated" poet; one knows why Mr. Eliot characterized Robinson as "negligible"; the direct attack is hardly the Eliot strategy.

Yet there are times and poems that put real questions and often imply real answers. Essentially, like any good poet, Robinson is less the philosopher than the metaphysician, and the question for him is the old ontological one. "The Man against the Sky" sums up the essence of Robinson's thought and feeling on the subject, thought and feeling which when they are working poetically prompt most of his best work, in both shorter lyrics and the poems of middle length. How does a man reconcile the idea of a beneficent, omnipotent God with the naked and frightening facts of existence? "What inexorable cause / Makes time so vicious in his reaping"? God or no God, for Robinson the true question is this: Is there a life after this one? If so, then it is all worth it, the suffering and the terror. If not, then why live? Yet in fact men do not often commit suicide, a phenomenon which Robinson seizes upon as a kind of proof that man does not end with the grave. Again and again, he will assert his belief in immortality and the ultimate importance of this life, while he utterly rejects materialism. Everywhere, in the poems, letters, and reported comment, such a deliberate choice of belief crops up, implied or stated. For all their polarities of style and rhetoric, "The Man against the Sky" and Wallace Stevens' "Sunday Morning" are complementary and classical views of the single question, and clearly emerge less from differing philosophies than from opposed temperaments. There is a will to doubt as well as to belief, and the existentialists' answer is not the only possible one. If truly philosophical influence on Robinson's views can be found, it seems clear, from Mr. Stevick's essay mentioned in the bibliography, that William James played the leading part in such influence. Yet even here it should be noted that James himself emphasizes that in dealing with such matters, he has entered the realm of metaphysics, and Robinson's discomfort under the rubric "philosopher" ought to be taken at least as seriously as any quasi-philosophical propositions he may seem to enunciate.

Robinson was a poet and poems are made with words, yet as a man so conspicuously of his century and heritage he was often at war with mere language and all unknowingly. By his own testimony it was words that fascinated him, that made and kept him a poet and a fine one, though the New Englander and the Victorian in him insisted that he must be the Seer, the Prophet, the Unacknowledged Legislator. Small wonder that in the direct conflict of these tendencies poetry is sometimes annihilated, and grist to the Ph.D. mill accumulates. This is not to say that Robinson had no mind and no ideas; it is simply that he mistook speculation in verse for poetic thought, as did unnumbered nineteenth-century writers before him. Still, each time he got a long poem out of his system and had as it were satisfied the Transcendental Philosopher in him, he could turn to real poetry again, and in *The Three Taverns* (1920) and *Avon's Harvest* (1921) he published some half-dozen of his best poems; even in the volume *Dionysius in Doubt* (1925), the last of his books containing short lyrics, there are two of his best sonnets, "New England" and "The Sheaves," and one or two others of real quality. But after that, there are only the long narratives, for the most part one each year up to his death. Of these, only *Ama-*

ranth would seem to bear repeated reading, and that in part for reasons not wholly artistic.

He had in a sense become a Man of Letters in the solid nineteenth-century sense of the term and the punctual appearance of a new volume seemed necessary to him — not, one supposes, because he needed the money as he himself claimed, but because publication, so long denied him, was both compensatory and reassuring. It made him as poet real to himself; when there was no book, there was no poet and no man, for rarely has an American poet lived in and for his work as did Robinson. One might say that apart from it, he had no life at all, at least after he went to New York to live. "If only they had said something about me! It would not have mattered what. They could have called me stupid or crazy if they liked. But they said nothing. Nobody devoted as much as an inch to me. I did not exist." If this, Robinson's own statement, is not absolutely true, it is near enough to full accuracy to convey the near-despair the poet must have felt during the years of total neglect. Friends helped, as did alcohol until it interfered with the poetry and then it was alcohol that had to go. But the lean years made a permanent and damaging mark on Robinson as poet, though they seem to have deepened his capacity as a man for the understanding of suffering, loneliness, and despair, as many of his letters testify. Deliberately reticent for fear of damaging self-exposure, he seems to have become more and more committed to one of his less attractive poetic characteristics, that of overqualification. Even in his letters, as apparently in conversation, his statements are frequently qualified by a deprecatory admission that the exact opposite may well be the case. Eventually this not unattractive personal quality is to become a stylistic tic and finally almost a major poetic device. In "Eros Turannos" we can note the modifying, qualifying lines and phrases. By the time of the long narratives, the tendency has solidified and we observe the not uncomon phenomenon of a poet's self-parody:

his complication of the simple and his propensity for giving to us for complex what is merely complicated and obscured, in other words, overqualified. These lines from *Cavender's House* (1929) illustrate the point:

> He knew there was a woman with two hands ·
> Watching him, but he saw no more of her
> Than would assure him she was there. He feared
> To see her face, and he feared not to see it;
> And then he found it as it was before,
> Languid and unrevealing. Her eyes closed,
> And her lips moved as if repeating words
> That had no meaning. . . .

Robinson tried, over a period of years, to write drama and fiction that should make some money — to no avail — and one suspects that in this case failure derived from a shortcoming he himself pointed out: he had no real subject. He later destroyed all his manuscripts of fiction, but two Ibsenite plays were published which leave no doubt that what is a bore in the poems is equally so in the plays. The truth is that the lack of a real subject in his later years, coupled with a growing inaptitude for straightforward storytelling, finally rendered narrative for the most part unavailable to him. The lines just quoted show how far he has come from the concrete and the sensuous and he will go even farther. Yet up until the last ten years of his life he was capable of first-rate work in various stanza forms, notably the sonnet.

Neglect, near-despair, and poverty had formed him and they worked themselves out to the bitter end even in the days of success. "Why don't they *read* me?" he would ask in mock despair. It was, and is, a good question and one surely that many a poet would like a fit answer to. They didn't read him because they did not like his tone of voice. For all that has been written of Robinson's originality, one is hard put to it to say precisely where the innovations lie.

He is simple. Yet his vocabulary is frequently polysyllabic and his metric jingly and derived. He seems rarely to be aware of the natural world or of the city, or if he does use the city as locale it is only in the vaguest, most perfunctory way as a stylized background. None of the qualities we associate with the Imagists, with Pound or Eliot, or with the ferment of the period is here, nor is there a trace of Frost's feeling for and against nature and rural New England. Even as serenely autumnal and lovely a poem as "Isaac and Archibald" lacks the specific and the minutely noted detail we think of as central to "nature poetry," whatever that may be. It is far closer to Wordsworth than to Frost and perhaps to Cowper than to either of the others in feeling. But one cannot read Robinson expecting certain things and find what he has to tell. If in his own time editors and others dismissed him because they thought his work grim and "pessimistic" they were at least nearer the right track than those who, enamored of the Great Rebellion, thought of him as a stuffy, mindless Yankee who had failed to get the word. The fact is, of course, that Robinson, between two movements and two worlds, could not be accepted by either. When triumph and commercial success came, they came late and for the most part in response to relatively inferior work.

Robinson loved words. Shy and almost wholly inarticulate in company, he wrote with great labor and with total absorption; not unexpectedly, therefore, he frequently confused best and worst in his work and failed to see where the logic of his own poetic intelligence took him. In his love of the involute and the tangential, he is kin to Henry James; in his fascination with language and metric, to Tennyson. But in his penetrating, naked vision of the reality that underlies human predicaments he seems close to the French novelists of the late nineteenth century and to Ibsen. He professed dislike of Flaubert and he sometimes inveighed against the sexual concern of many of the naturalists, yet Zola and Whitman cast a spell on him, however briefly. Kipling's capacity to make poetry out of the commonplace interested and excited him, but more than all of these there was a Yankee eclecticism of language that made him go anywhere for words that would when pressed together make something hard, curious, and impenetrable. Milton, Shakespeare, Browning, Crabbe, Tennyson, Cowper, and a host of Romantics supply part of the vocabulary and the subject matter a vocabulary discovers for itself.

And what is the subject? the temper of it and the tone in which it comes to us? "When the stars are shining blue / There will yet be left a few / Themes availing — / And these failing, / Momus, there'll be you." Here is one of the faces of his Muse, and another was Pity; not tenderness or really what we would call sympathy, but pity for poor souls caught in the trap that their own weakness and fate have combined to spring. Viewed from the modern point of view, many of the best poems lack what is called compassion, as witness the destruction of Pink, Miss Watchman, and Atlas in *Amaranth*. We somehow demand that the poet express a feeling for the fates of his doomed victims. Robinson will not gratify the common expectations, for he is concerned to show the plight and to imply the terror and the rigor of the doom — a doom, one sees, both merited and gratuitous. When this fate is a secretion from the poem and not its nominal subject, the poem is likely to be terse, packed, and utterly objective: the poet presents certain people in certain predicaments and tells what happened. In nearly every case we can see that the issue is one of illusion overcoming the sense of reality. At times illusion is shown as something a character wills and achieves; a state which the person deliberately chooses as preferable to actuality or as providing the only alternative to suicide. Job's wife, Robinson implies, is the stern realist and recommends to Job that he "curse God and die." She has seized "the swift logic of a woman." But though many of Robinson's fated creatures do indeed doom themselves by failing to "see," as he puts it, there are occasionally those who, staking their lives and honors on "illusions," come through triumphantly.

Conrad might have understood these poems had he known them. For Robinson as for Conrad, illusion is the very stuff of living and the naked realist is either the complete and successful Romantic, or a suicide. Illusion is willed and forced into some kind of reality, or it is escape. And in the latter case, it will eventually destroy its slave. The mother in "The Gift of God" forces her wholly inaccurate dream of her son's worth into what is for her the realm of fact which nothing can violate because it rests on limitless unselfish love. The wife in "Eros Turannos" has chosen to deceive herself but has reached a point at which the extent of the deception and its origins are about to reveal themselves — with destruction inevitable. In "Veteran Sirens" the women who "cry out for time to end his levity" have discovered that the joke is on them and not on anyone else; the wife of "The Mill" needs only to know what she knows and to have heard her husband say "There are no millers any more." After that, what else can happen than does?

In creating his effects of fate and of "levity," Robinson relies heavily on a hard surface of objective statement, an intermittent current of humor — from gentle to sardonic — and a metric that seems frequently at odds with the subject matter, as though a pastoral elegy should be set to the tune of "Jingle Bells." The tripping, sometimes metronomic, measure alternates with sonorities, as the language alternates between the homely phrase and the "grand manner." In "Mr. Flood's Party" we see a similar technique in imagery: the juxtaposition of the grand and the ordinary, Eben Flood with his jug of hard cider to his lips "like Roland's ghost, winding a silent horn." The image and the language are at once evocative, original, and straight out of the tradition. And they are meant to be, for the "larger humor of the thing" as Robinson says in another place. The very objectivity with which Robinson views his destroyed and self-destroying characters allows him to forgo compassion and to present their plights with humor while he never shirks the rigor and the pity of the particular destiny. It is an appeal to us, as readers, to apply the same technique to our own capacities for self-deception, to see ourselves as "the clerks of time" or to watch "great oaks return / To acorns out of which they grew." The humor and levity arise from Robinson's refusal, when he is at his best, to consider human error as necessarily cosmically tragic. His Captain Craig, indomitable in defeat and death, is in fact a failure not only in the world's eyes, but in the eyes of the perceptive beholder and perhaps in his own too. And of course Robinson implies that all men are failures in this sense; "poets and kings are but the clerks of time." Hence "the larger humor," the levity, can be felt only by sensibilities realistic enough to understand their own plights and to relate those plights to the whole human condition.

Of course, there are occasions and poems when this sort of humor will not do, will not answer the call of a spirit too appalled at the workings of fate to achieve the right tone. In much of Robinson's work there is another face to the god of reality and understanding. Some facts are too horrible to face and too gratuitously violent for understanding. Poems like "For a Dead Lady" and "The Mill" belong to this category. In the former there is no attempt whatever at mitigating the horror or at achieving acceptance or understanding. Such things are simply *there*. To understand would be to play God; to accept would be demonic. On the whole, this side of the Robinsonian subject is less common than the former; it is not, for example, commonly to be seen at all in the longer poems, where frequently violent acts, often perverted acts, create denouement or tragic conflict almost as though violence has for Robinson taken the place of what might be termed the irrational principle in life. In *Lancelot* and *Amaranth*, to cite two of Robinson's best long narratives, understanding, acceptance, and the promise of a new life form the very basis of the subject and the theme, but it must be confessed that some of Robinson's finest work moves in the direction of stating or implying that at the center of our existence is something implacable, irrational, and not to be propitiated. The old cliché often used of Robinson that he celebrated the success of failure and the failure of success has only a limited application, notable in such a poem as "Old Trails"; actually, he found little reward in failure as such, nor do his failures like Captain Craig and Eben Flood in any sense "triumph"; they are as deluded as the man who congratulates himself on his success. Men fall short of essential humanity and it is here that Robinson's irony usually comes into play, in poems which treat of people in particular situations which show them as inadequate to the human demands made upon them. These poems have plot, action, place, and time; they nearly always involve a man or a woman who is confronted with a situation, involving others, which demands a radical reappraisal of the self and one's conduct. The character is called upon to discard a cherished image of himself, and nearly always, in refusing or failing to do so, the character suffers disaster.

In order to see how Robinson works out the fates of such people in such poems, it might be well to look closely at two or three of the best examples and try to see what goes on. The best poems of the sort described have a dense, deceptive surface, organized in a seemingly careful, orderly way and proceeding quietly, baldly almost, while the narrator subtly assumes the point of view of the reader and imperceptibly helps him to assess and understand, finally leaving with him the realization that the ending is both inevitable and wholly human. The following analyses, then, attempt to show how certain of Robinson's best poems, each representative of a different aspect of the Robinsonian subject, achieve the desired effect.

"Eros Turannos" unfolds as narrative, compressed and suggestive yet without the trickery that occasionally irritates us, as in the case of "The Whip" or "How Annandale Went Out." Most noticeably, the language is general, the tone expository, the purpose of the poem communication rather than expression. Adumbrated in the first stanza, certain images, whose latent power and meanings are reserved until the final lines, have the function of motifs, repeated constantly and expanded as the poem opens out into suggestion. There are three such images or symbols: waves, tree, stairs leading down. Throughout, these symbols control and provide a center for the meanings possible to the poem, and from the mention of "downward years" and "foamless weirs" in the first stanza to the triple vision of the last four lines these elements recur, the same but altered. As is the case with so many Robinson poems, the reader must supply, from the general materials provided, his own construction, yet the poet has seen to it that there can be only one possible final product. The poem contains two complementary parts: the abstract, generalized statement and the symbolic counterpart of that statement, each constituting a kind of gloss upon the other; each moves through the poem parallel to the other, until at the end they become fused in the concrete images. In addition to the three symbols mentioned, we find also that of blindness and dimness, summed up in the single word "veil" yet continually present in the words "mask," "blurred," "dimmed," "fades," "illusion." All this culminates in the sweeping final image: "Or like a stairway to the sea / Where down the blind are driven." Yet such inner order, such tight articulation as these examples may indicate, derives no more from the concrete than from the generalized; contrary to Marianne Moore's professed belief, not all imaginary gardens need have actual toads in them, nor, conversely, do we have to bother with the toad at all if our garden is imagined truly enough. What we must have is room — for toads or non-toads, but room anyhow, and Robinson seems to say that there will be more room if we don't clutter the garden with too many particular sorts of fauna and flora. For in "Eros Turannos" we are not told the where or the wherefore; only, and it is everything, the how and the just so. In the hinted-at complexity of the woman's emotion, in the suggested vagueness of the man's worthlessness, lies the whole history of human trust and self-deception: none shall see this incident for what it really is, and the woman who hides her trouble has as much of the truth as "we" who guess and guess, yet, the poem implies, without coming nearer to the truth than men usually do.

"Eros Turannos" is the Robinsonian archetype, for in it we can find the basic elements, the structural pattern, that he was to use frequently and with large success. The most cursory reading affords a glimpse into the potential power as well as the dangers of such a form; Robinson's use of it provides examples of both. In the poem in question he reaches an ultimate kind of equipoise of statement and suggestion, generalization and concretion. The first three words of the poem set the tone, provide the key to a "plot" which the rest will set before us. "She fears him": simple statement; what follows will explore the statement, and we shall try to observe the method and evaluate its effect.

> She fears him, and will always ask
>   What fated her to choose him;
> She meets in his engaging mask
>   All reasons to refuse him;
> But what she meets and what she fears
> Are less than are the downward years,
> Drawn slowly to the foamless weirs
>   Of age, were she to lose him.

The epigrammatic tone of the verse strikes one immediately; we are aware that here is a kind of expository writing, capable in its generality of evoking a good deal more than the words state. Important though unobtrusive imagery not only reinforces and enriches the exposition but by calculated ambiguity as well sets a tone of suspense and fatality. The man wears a mask: he conceals something that at once repels and attracts her; notice the play on "engaging" and the implications that involves. The motif is an important one for the poem, as is that contained in the metaphor of "weirs," since these two suggestions of deception, distrust, entrapment, blindness, and decline will be continually alluded to throughout the poem, to find an ultimate range of meaning in the final lines.

The second stanza will in such expressions as "blurred" and "to sound" keep us in mind of the motifs mentioned, without actually requiring new imagistic material or forcing us to re-imagine the earlier metaphors. The intent here is not to be vague but to retain in the reader's consciousness what has gone before as that consciousness acquires new impressions. Hence, in stanza three, Robinson can now introduce a suggestive sketch of the man's nature while he reminds of the woman's and continues to explore it:

> A sense of ocean and old trees
> Envelops and allures him;
> Tradition, touching all he sees,
> Beguiles and reassures him;

That engaging mask of his becomes apparent to us here in this man who finds a solace and security in the love of his wife and in her solid place in the community, and yet the sinister note first sounded in the image of "weirs" is lightly alluded to in the phrase "a sense of ocean." Moreover, that he too is "beguiled" presents a possibility of irony beyond what has yet been exploited.

> And all her doubts of what he says
> Are dimmed with what she knows of days —
> Till even prejudice delays
> And fades, and she secures him.

The possibilities are many. We grasp readily enough the pathos of her situation: a woman with a worthless husband, proud and sensitive to what the town is whispering yet ready to submit to any indignity, to close her eyes and ears, rather than live alone. Surely a common enough theme in American writing and one that allows the poet to suggest rather than dramatize. Again, in "dimmed" we catch an echo of what has gone before, and in the last two lines the abstract noun "prejudice" with its deliberately general verbs "delays" and "fades" presents no image but rather provokes the imagination to a vision of domestic unhappiness familiar to us all, either in fiction or empirically. And of course the finality of "secures," ironic neither in itself nor in its position in the stanza, takes on irony when we see what such security must be: the woman finds peace only by blinding herself and by seeing the man as she wishes to see him.

Stanza four once again recapitulates and explores. Statement alternates with image, the inner suffering with the world's vision of it:

> And home, where passion lived and died,
> Becomes a place where she can hide,
> While all the town and harbor side
> Vibrate with her seclusion.

If this stanza forms the climax of the plot, so to speak, the next comes to a kind of stasis, the complication of events and motives and themes we see so often in Henry James. The outside world of critical townspeople, hinted at before, now comes to the foreground, and we get a complication of attitudes and views — the world's, the woman's, the man's, our own — and the poet's is ours too. Yet even in a passage as seemingly prosaic and bare as this Robinson keeps us mindful of what has gone before. In stanza four such words as "falling," "wave," "illusion," "hide," and "harbor" have served to keep us in mind of the various themes as well as to advance the plot, and in the fifth stanza Robinson presents us with a series of possible views of the matter, tells us twice that this is a "story," reiterates that deception and hiding are the main themes, as in the metaphorical expression "veil" and in the simple statement "As if the story of a house / Were told, or ever could be." And at last, in the final lines, thematic, narrative, and symbolic materials merge in the three images that accumulate power as they move from the simple to the complex, from the active to the passive, from the less to the more terrible:

> Though like waves breaking it may be,
> Or like a changed familiar tree,
> Or like a stairway to the sea
> Where down the blind are driven.

For the attentive reader the narrative cannot fail; Robinson has given us the suggestive outline we need and told us how, in general, to think about this story. He has kept us constantly aware of place, time, actors, and action even though such awareness is only lightly provoked and not insisted on. In the last stanza the curious downward flow of the poem, the flow of the speculation, reaches an ultimate debouchment—"where down the blind are driven." Apart from the metrical power, the movement of the poem is significant; Robinson has packed it with words that suggest descent, depth, and removal from sight, so that the terrible acceptance of the notion that we must "take what the god has given" becomes more terrible, more final as it issues out in the logic of statement and imagery and in the logic of the plot.

If much of the poem's power depends upon the interaction of statement and suggestion, still another source of energy is the metric. Robinson here uses a favorite device of his, feminine rhymes, in alternating tetrameter and trimeter lines, and gives to soft-sounding, polysyllabic words important metrical functions; as a result, when he does invert a foot or wrench the rhythm or use a monosyllable, the effect is striking out of all proportion to its apparent surface value. Surely the plucking, sounding quality of the word "vibrate" in the last line of the fourth stanza is proof of this, though equally effective is the position of "down" and "blind" in the final line of the poem.

Contemporary verse has experimented with meters, rhyme, and rhythm to such an extent that one has to attune the ear to Robinson's verse; at first it sounds jingly and mechanical, perhaps inept, but after we make a trial of them, the skill, the calculation, have their way and the occasional deviations from the set pattern take on the greater power because they are deviations:

> Pity, I learned, was not the least
> Of time's offending benefits
> That had now for so long impugned
> The conservation of his wits:
> Rather it was that I should yield,
> Alone, the fealty that presents
> The tribute of a tempered ear
> To an untempered eloquence.

This stanza from "The Wandering Jew" shows the style. This is mastery of prosody — old-fashioned command of the medium. The reversing of feet, use of alternately polysyllabic and monosyllabic words, of syncopation ("To an untempered eloquence") are devices subtly and sparingly used. The last stanza of the same poem gives another instance, and here the running-on of the sense through three and a half lines adds to the effect:

> Whether he still defies or not
> The failure of an angry task
> That relegates him out of time
> To chaos, I can only ask.
> But as I knew him, so he was;
> And somewhere among men to-day
> Those old, unyielding eyes may flash,
> And flinch — and look the other way.

Deviation implies a basic pattern, and although in many cases, particularly in the blank-verse narratives, syllable-counting mars the prosody, nonetheless the best poems subtly attune themselves to the "tempered ear," syncopate on occasion, and jingle to good effect.

This analysis is technical and only partial; it seems to presuppose that we must lapse into Cleanth Brooks's "heresy of paraphrase." Granted. Yet this but begs a question, inasmuch as all of Robinson's poetry assumes that one will want to find the paraphrasable element the poet has carefully provided. These are poems *about* something, and what the something is we must discover. That is why we should consider Robinson as a poet with a prose in view; to read "Eros Tu-rannos" or "For a Dead Lady" or "The Gift of God" is to feel that the scope of a long naturalistic novel has emerged from a few stanzas. Yet Allen Tate, in a brief essay, says that Robinson's lyrics are "dramatic" and that T. S. Eliot observes this to be a characteristic of the best modern verse. One is really at a loss to know what the word "dramatic" means in this regard; Robinson's poetry is not dramatic in any sense of the word commonly accepted, unless it be that Robinson, like Henry James, frequently unfolds a scene. To look for anything like drama in the poems is idle, in that the excitement they convey is of a muted sort, akin to that which James himself generates. This poet wears no masks; he is simply at a distance from his poem, unfolding the "plot," letting us see and letting us make what applications we will. This directness, this prose element, in Robinson's verse is easy enough to find; less so to define or characterize. One can say this, however: just as Pope was at his best in a poetry that had morality and man in society as its subject matter and its criterion, so Robinson is happiest as a poet when he starts with a specific human situation or relationship, with a "story." "Eros Tu-rannos" is *about* the marriage of untrue minds, but specifically it is not about just untrueness and minds; it is about untrue man A and suffering, self-deluding woman B, as well as about those worldly wisemen who conjecture and have all the "dope." Usually unsuccessful in speculative verse, Robinson excels in just this naturalistic

31

case-history, this story of a Maine Emma Bovary. If the theme is still failure, Robinson rings a peculiar change upon it, since at last the poem forces us to accept the implication that there *is* and must be a "kindly veil between / Her visions and those we have seen"; that all of us must "take what the god has given," for failure is, in Robinson's world, the condition of man and human life. We do the best we can. In "Old Trails," the best one can is not often good, and what is indeed success in the world's eyes has a very shoddy look to those who recognize the success as merely "a safer way / Than growing old alone among the ghosts." It is the success of Chad in James's *The Ambassadors*, who will go home to the prosperous mills and Mamie and Mom, not that of Strether, who could have had the money and the ease but took the way of "growing old among the ghosts."

A briefer, more compact poem than "Old Trails," one that deals with another aspect of the theme, is the sonnet "The Clerks," which for all its seeming spareness is a very rich, very deft performance. The octave opens colloquially, gives us a general location and an unspecified number of clerks; the speaker is the poet, as poet and as man. Robinson draws an evocative, generalized sketch of the clerks' past, of their prime as well as of the slow attrition of time and labor, and affirms that despite the wear they have sustained these men are still good and human. It is in the sestet that the poem moves out into suggestion, that it implies a conceit by which we can see how all men are clerks, time-servers, who are subject to fears and visions, who are high and low, and who as they tier up also cut down and trim away. To call the poem a conceit is no mere exercise of wit, for Robinson has clearly punned on many unobtrusive words in the sonnet. What is the clerks' "ancient air"? Does it mean simply that the men are old and tired? or that their manner is one of recalling grand old times of companionship that never really existed? or that one must take "air" literally to mean their musty smell of the store? These possibilities are rendered the more complex by the phrase "shopworn brotherhood" immediately following, for then the visual element is reinforced, the atmosphere of shoddiness and shabbiness, of Rotary club good-fellowship, and the simple language has invested itself with imagistic material that is both olfactory and visual. And of course, one may well suspect sarcasm in the assertion that "the men were just as good, / And just as human as they ever were." How good were they? Yet lest anyone feel this is too cynical, Robinson carefully equates the clerks with "poets and kings."

As is the case with "Eros Turannos," this poem proceeds from the general to the specific and back to the general again, a generality now enlarged to include comment on and a kind of definition of the human condition. Throughout there have been ironic overtones, ironic according to the irony we have seen as peculiarly Robinsonian in that it forms one quadrant of the total view. It has to do here with the discrepancy between the vision men have of their lives and the actuality they have lived. The poet here implies that such discrepancy, such imperfection of vision is immutably "human" and perhaps therefore, and ironically, "good." That the clerks (and we are all clerks) see themselves as at once changed and the same, "fair" yet only called so, serves as the kind of lie men exist by, a lie that becomes an "ache" on the one hand and the very nutriment that supports life on the other. You, all you who secretly cherish some irrational hope or comfort, merely "feed yourselves with your descent," your ancestry, your career, your abject position miscalled a progress. For all of us there can be only the wastage, the building up to the point of dissatisfaction, the clipping away to the point of despair.

Despite the almost insupportable rigor of Robinson's attitude, we can hardly accuse him of cynicism or of hopelessness. In every instance his view of people is warm and understanding, not as the patronizing seer but as the fellow-sufferer. Such feeling informs the poems we have discussed and fills "The Gift of God" with humanity no cynic could imagine, no despair encompass. For in this poem the

33

theme of failure turns once more, this time in an unexpected way so that we see Robinson affirming self-deception of this specific kind as more human, more the gauge of true love than all the snide fact-finding the rest of the world would recommend. The poem is about a mother's stubborn, blind love for a worthless (or perhaps merely ordinary) son, and this in the teeth of all the evidence her neighbors would be delighted to retail. Again, the poem is a compact narrative; again the irony exists outside the poem, not in its expression. As in so many of the best poems, Robinson says in effect: here is the reality, here is the illusion. *You* compare them and say which is which and if possible which is the correct moral choice.

The metaphorical material we can roughly classify as made up of imagery relating to royalty, apotheosis, sacrifice, and love. From the first few lines we are aware of a quality which, by allusion to the Annunciation and the anointing of kings, establishes the mother's cherished illusion and thereby makes acceptance of the emergent irony inescapably the reader's duty; he must compare the fact and the fiction for and by himself; Robinson will not say anything in such a way as to make the responsibility for choice his own rather than the reader's. He will simply render the situation and leave us to judge it, for all of Robinson's poems presuppose an outside world of critics and judges, of ourselves, people who see and observe more or less clearly. His irony is external; it lies in the always hinted-at conflict between the public life and the private, between the thing seen from the inside and from the outside, with the poet, the speaker, presenting a third vision, not one that reconciles or cancels the other two, but one which simply adds a dimension and shows us that "everything is true in a different sense."

If the dominant motifs in "The Gift of God" are as indicated above, the progression of the poem follows undeviatingly the pattern suggested. In the first stanza Annunciation; the second, Nativity; the third, vision; the fourth, a stasis in which the mother seems to accept her son's unusual merit and her own vision of him as real; the fifth, a further extension of vision beyond anything actual; the sixth, the culmination of this calculated vision in the apotheosis. More than a schematized structure, the poem depends not only on the articulation of motifs and a plot, but equally on symbolic material that interacts with the stated or implied events in the "plot." Thus, from the outset the poet has juxtaposed the illusory vision and the "firmness" of the mother's faith in it; the language has a flavor of vague association with kingship, biblical story, and legend, notably conveyed by such words as "shining," "degree," "anointed," "sacrilege," "transmutes," and "crowns." Yet in the careful arrangement of his poem Robinson has not oversimplified the mother's attitude. She maintains her "innocence unwrung" (and the irony of the allusion is not insisted on) despite the common knowledge of people who know, of course, better, and Robinson more than implies the innocence of her love in the elevated yet unmetaphorical diction he uses. Not until the final stanza does he open the poem out, and suddenly show the apotheosis in the image of "roses thrown on marble stairs," subtly compressing into the last three lines the total pathos of the poem, for the son ascending in the mother's dream is "clouded" by a "fall": the greatness his mother envisions is belied by what we see. And who is in the right? For in the final turn of the "plot," is it not the mother who gives the roses of love and the marble of enduring faith? Is the dream not as solid and as real as human love can make it? If we doubt this notion, we need only observe the value Robinson places on the verb "transmutes" in stanza five: "*Transmutes* him with her faith and praise." She has, by an absolute miracle of alchemy, transmuted base material into precious; by an act of faith, however misplaced, found the philosopher's stone, which is love wholly purged of self.

What we have come to realize is that in these poems we have been considering we are concerned with narrative — narrative of a peculiar kind in which the story is not just about the events, people, and relationships but about the very poetic devices which are the vehicle of the narration and its insights. In "The Gift of God" symbol and theme have a narrative function; they must do in brief and without obtrusiveness what long passages of dialogue, exposition, and description would effect in a novel. As a result, the reader is compelled to take the entire poem in at once; he either "understands" it or he does not. Naturally there are subtleties which emerge only after many readings; yet because these poems are narratives, Robinson must concentrate upon communication, upon giving us a surface that is at once dense yet readily available to the understanding.

> As one apart, immune, alone,
> Or featured for the shining ones,
> And like to none that she has known
> Of other women's other sons,—
> The firm fruition of her need,
> He shines anointed; and he blurs
> Her vision, till it seems indeed
> A sacrilege to call him hers.

This is on one hand simple telling of plot: the mother sees her son as unique and feels unworthy to be his mother. Simple enough. But the story is more than this, more than a cold telling of the facts about the mother's vision of her son. We see on the other hand that it is her need of the son, and of the vision of him, which complicates the story, while the suggestion of kingship, ritual, and sacrifice in the diction, with the implication of self-immolation and deception, further extends the possibilities of meaning.

All this we grasp more readily than we may realize, for Robinson prepares for his effects very early and while he extends meaning is careful to recapitulate, to restate and re-emphasize the while he varies and complicates:

> She sees him rather at the goal,
> Still shining; and her dream foretells
> The proper shining of a soul
> Where nothing ordinary dwells.

In these lines Robinson affirms the mother's illusion — it is a "dream" that "foretells"— and recapitulates the theme of kingship, of near-divinity, in the repetition of "shining." The stanza that follows gives the poem its turn, states specifically that the son is merely ordinary, that the mother deludes herself, that her motive in so doing is "innocent," and in stanza five the poem, as we have seen, turns once more, pivots on the verb "transmute," turns away from the simple ironical comparison we have been experiencing and reveals a transmuted relationship: son to mother, vision to fact, and an ultimate apotheosis of the mother under the guise of a mistaken view of the son. The poem is about all these things and is equally about the means of their accomplishment within the poem. This is a poetry of surfaces, dense and deceptive surfaces to be sure but still a poetry that insists on the communication of a whole meaning, totally and at once:

> She crowns him with her gratefulness,
> And says again that life is good;
> And should the gift of God be less
> In him than in her motherhood,
> His fame, though vague, will not be small,
> As upward through her dream he fares,
> Half clouded with a crimson fall
> Of roses thrown on marble stairs.

The recapitulation, the tying together, of the symbolic and thematic materials serves in this, the last stanza, a narrative as well as an expressive purpose. The tone is epigrammatic rather than prosaic and must shift delicately, come to the edge of banality, then turn off and finally achieve a muted sublimity that runs every risk of sentimentality and rhetoric yet never falters. The verse requires of us what it requires of itself: a toughness that can encompass the trite and mawkish without on the one hand turning sentimental itself or on the other resorting to an easy irony. The technique is the opposite of dramatic in that Robinson leaves as much to the reader as he possibly can; he uses no persona; the conflict-in-action before our eyes, as it unfolds itself at once, passes through complications, and returns to the starting point, the same yet altered and, to some degree, understood. To this extent Robinson is ratiocinative rather than dramatic; what we and the characters themselves think about the "plot" is as important as the plot, becomes indeed the full meaning of the plot.

Here, again, Robinson is likely to seem behind the times to certain readers. The narrative mode is unpopular in contemporary verse, and even poems about people who are not legendary or at least historical seem to be out of fashion. But the form is an old and honorable one with practitioners as variously gifted as Crabbe, Chaucer, Skelton, Prior, Tennyson, Browning, Kipling, certain Pre-Raphaelites and Decadents, a not inconsiderable company. And Wordsworth made a form of his own of it. Nearly always, the temptation is to move to the long narrative, the viability of which in recent decades is a vexed question. Nonetheless, however strongly dramatic monologue persists in our own era, the narrative lyric has largely disappeared, largely because of the tendency of most modern poetry to be, on the one hand, abstract, philosophical, didactic, or, on the other, rhapsodic, quasi-mystical, symbolist. Certain of the best practitioners in each mode transcend boundaries and mingle the two; one thinks of Stevens and Yeats here. But a Hart Crane, a Dylan Thomas, a Pound: these poets have a particular country from which they rarely stray with success. Robinson had, of course, a historical and local advantage: the nineteenth century was still available to him as an influence and a source, and his upbringing served to keep him isolated, during his formative years, from a too-doctrinaire rejection of his heritage. There is a disadvantage in rebellion and experiment, as there is in indiscriminate acceptance. Robinson took over much Romantic feeling and practice because it suited him. What did not suit him in it was its diction, its remoteness from real experience, and its mere rhetoric. For him, the narrative lyric represented an eclectic form combining many sorts of Romantic poetry, but with the superaddition of a new vocabulary, a sense of real life in a particular time and place, and a zeal for solid truth. Hence his deliberate omission from *Tristram* of the love-potion. That was too much to swallow!

For all that has been said of the shorter poems, we are still left with the vexed question of the blank-verse narratives, the longer and the shorter. Clearly, any attentive reader will single out for first place among the latter such poems as "Isaac and Archibald," "Aunt Imogen," "Rembrandt to Rembrandt," and "The Three Taverns." All are notable for the absence of that garrulity which grew on Robinson, particularly in the last decade of his life, as well as for their structure and genuine intellectual content: in them Robinson thinks as a poet doing a job of work should think. The first is a New England pastoral, muted yet rich in tone, gently ironic yet lyrical, and marked by the poet's characteristic humorous self-deprecation as well as his insight into both youth and age. The second poem, less ambitious perhaps, is a marvel of escape from a trap that seems to promise certain capture in sentimentality; it is the story of an old maid who finds her annual emotional release in a month's stay with her sister and her children. What saves the poem is its utter honesty of feeling and language; the poem is not about pathos — pathos simply leaks out of the plain account the poet gives. But "Rembrandt to Rembrandt," a more ambitious piece, addresses itself to the problem of the solitary artist and in so doing is even more intimately autobiographical in feeling than the others. Again, the poem never makes the mistake of being about its own emotions; Robinson here concentrates on the artist's agonized yet sardonic assessment of his own plight. There is no solution, no dedication to the higher aims; only the realization that he moves among demons of self-doubt, self-delusion, and self-pity. Something of the same kind appears in "The Three Taverns" in which St. Paul seems to be analyzing for us the relative importance of faith and the Law. And here Robinson, abandoning a heritage of Calvinism and a more recent tradition of Puritan fideism, comes out strongly, in the persona of Paul, for a faith at once personal and from authority, ruled finally by wisdom slowly and painstakingly acquired. There are to be few sudden visions and visitations and those only for the elect.

If the foregoing remarks indicate, as they should, that in these shorter narratives Robinson is doing the poet's work with economy, high intelligence, and skill, what is to follow must of necessity show the other side of the coin. One must say candidly that with the exception of parts of the Arthurian cycle and of *Amaranth*, all the later long narratives are arid, badly thought out, and, as it were, tired. The reasons for this decay appear earlier and there is no need to rehearse them. Briefly, however, here are some of the qualities which these long poems show.

Merlin (1917), *Lancelot* (1920), and *Tristram* (1927) make up the Arthurian cycle and for all their failings surely treat the epic Arthurian theme with greater meaning and importance than do any other works of modern times, T. H. White's possibly excepted. The poems are of course allegorical in conception, at least in the case of the first two, and *Lancelot* really comes close to maintaining a successful interplay of the actual and the symbolic on an extended scale. Yet we have to admit that Robinson's besetting sins, the over-elaboration of the obvious and whimsical garrulity, always potential in his work, here begin to exert their fatal influence. Everything Robinson wrote in blank verse in the last fifteen or twenty years of his life is too long, too diffuse, too manneristic. One feels that, like James, Robinson began to enjoy his own work too much, the sound of his own voice tended to intoxicate him. But enough — there are superb passages in *Merlin* and the characters of Vivian and Merlin are real and believable; Lancelot, Arthur, and Guinevere are also powerfully imagined, particularly Lancelot in the poem of that name. If Gawain is hopelessly tedious with the tedious whimsy that grew on Robinson, the figure of Lancelot emerges as heroic, human yet larger than life, a great soldier and a man of noble nature.

Fundamentally, the weakness of the whole cycle derives from Robinson's uneasy poetic and structural compromise: here is myth, symbol, allegory, yet here equally are men and women of the twentieth century. Reconciliation of these disparate parts is, if not impossible, at least an immensely formidable task. Robinson comes close to success in *Lancelot* only because myth, symbol, and allegory disappear when the poem is at its best and we have the powerfully conveyed triangular affair of Arthur, Guinevere, and Lancelot. In *Tristram* — Robinson's great popular success — there is much lyric beauty but the poem is fatally flawed by a love affair at once sticky and verbose and by characters more reminiscent of routine historical novels than of men and women out of myth and legend. And the later narratives, though perhaps less embarrassing in their portrayals of love and lovers, do fatally remind one of *Redbook*, if only in the names of the heroines: Laramie, Gabrielle, Natalie, Karen. Only *Amaranth*, in returning to the old subject of failure and self-delusion in artists, touches reality and by fits and starts finds life and meaning. Robinson's last poem, *King Jasper* (1935), is another raid on the abstract by way of allegory and shows the poet's exhaustion — he was on his deathbed when it was completed — as do perhaps to some extent all these late narratives. "A series of conversations terminated by an accident." This dismissal of Ibsen's *A Doll's House* quoted by Yeats might serve to characterize the general effect of these poems on the modern reader, and if it seems sweeping and harsh, any qualifications can serve only to mitigate the judgment, not revoke it.

Yet Robinson stands alone among American poets in his devotion to the long poem. *Captain Craig* remains unique in our annals, rivaled in England by one or two of John Masefield's. In the narrative poem of moderate length, like "Isaac and Archibald," there is no one to touch him; Wordsworth's "Michael" and Keats's "Lamia" would seem the sole competitors in the genre throughout modern times. Robinson of course precedes Frost, in both time and originality, as a writer of short narratives. Frost's "The Death of the Hired Man," for example, lacks both the verbal complexity and the metrical subtlety of Robinson; when Frost turns to such a poem as "Out, Out," however, he is on firm ground indeed where none can outdo him. Both poets clearly find the compressed, elliptically told story their "supreme fiction." It is entirely possible that certain readers can never bring themselves to enjoy verse of this sort — muted, ironic, understated. For some, Robinson is less exciting than, say, Wallace Stevens, born only ten years after Robinson, just as Coleridge seems to many readers more exciting than Wordsworth, Hopkins more daring and absorbing than Tennyson. One might put it this way: Robinson in his best work has no specific religious or philosophical position to recommend, as neither Keats nor Wordsworth has; Hopkins, Stevens, Pound — these are poets who want to sell us something, a theory, a set of ideas or principles. If we like the principles we will love the poetry. For some, Robinson has a defect which goes far, in their view, to cancel out most if not all of his great merit; there is a certain dryness and mechanicalness of tone and feeling which for certain readers will always be an insuperable obstacle, as the "egotistical-sublime" of Wordsworth will always limit his audience. The reader who likes "Michael" will probably like "Isaac and Archibald." Robinson writes about himself in a guise some of us can recognize and enjoy; he does not pose, he does not try to give opinions. Personality in a poet is of the essence. We must like him as he speaks to us or we had better not read him.

That his poetic personality included a strong lyrical element cannot be denied, though it is frequently overlooked, largely because the poet rarely indulged it. We have seen that it was at least once overindulged in *Tristram* and we know that Robinson often kept it in reserve that its appearance might have the greater effect. The language, the imagery, of this lyricism derive largely from nineteenth-century sources, as in the opening lines of "The Man against the Sky" in which poem, as in "The Dark Hills," a deliberate use of highly colored rhetoric is central to the purpose. Unlike many poets of recent years, Robinson was not afraid of lyricism, nor, unlike still others, did he try to overwhelm the reader with "original" and striking imagery. The image of Eben Flood like "Roland's ghost winding a silent horn" is a typical example of one kind of Robinsonian lyricism in that it is euphonious, nostalgic, traditional — and wittily ironic.

But not all Robinson's lyrical flights are of these two sorts, the rhetorical or the ironic. Many occur as climaxes to poems which have begun in a muted, somber tone, rise gradually and reach a peak of grandeur and eloquence in the final lines. We can observe the technique in such poems as "The White Lights," "On the Night of a Friend's Wedding," "The Sheaves," and of course, "The Gift of God." But there are still those poems which are primarily, almost purely, lyrical, and though few critics think of Robinson as a lyricist, or even as a poet of great versatility, a thorough reading of his work discloses a number of fine poems of quiet but powerful lyric intensity. "Luke Havergal" is one, a poem of almost macabre symbolism. Others, like "Pasa Thalassa Thalassa" and "The Wilderness," with their overtones of Kipling and Swinburne, seem Pre-Raphaelite in quality, as does the "Villanelle of Change." There remains nonetheless the conviction that Robinson's greatest triumphs and happiest effects derive from the "mixed" lyric, the poem rooted in situation which combines narrative, lyrical and ironic, often humorous, qualities with the intent of creating a more complex emotional state in the reader than that effected by the "pure" lyric. "The House on the Hill," "Veteran Sirens," "John Evereldown," and "New England," all display in their differing accents and rhythms the possibilities of this "mixed" form. Wit, pathos, lyrical power, and understatement combine in varied ways to produce complex states of feeling. It is one of the truly Robinsonian characteristics which can be called both modern and highly personal, characteristic of the man and the manner.

Finally, it must be avowed that any writer with a marked manner — and Robinson's manner is strongly marked — offends certain sensibilities, and those often the most acute. The defects and virtues of a poet are so closely allied that frequently they go hand in hand and it takes many bad poems to generate one good one. Robinson's fault was of course to mistake the attempt for the achieved thing. Can anyone say Robinson is alone in such misapprehension? We have seen the damaging effects on Robinson of exile from the kind of give-and-take the knowledge of the better contemporary minds can provide. He had protected his one talent so long and under such stress that we cannot wonder that he took little advice and criticism when it came to him. He was not a Browning; his latter days were divided between the MacDowell Colony in the summers, New York, and visits to friends and to "Tilbury Town," whither he now came as her most famous son — and can we imagine what that must have done to his long-battered pride? But he was not spoiled. He did not surround himself with doting women, or go to tea-fights and give readings — he shrank from these with horror, and a touch of cynicism. He kept on writing, as we have seen, and writing increasingly to satisfy, perhaps to justify, a conception of himself as poet and as man. The great fault of the nineteenth-century men of letters was to publish everything, and Robinson was of his time in this as in so much else. But his successes are many and large — in the narrative poem, the sonnet, the reflective lyric, the narrative lyric, and the dramatic monologue. Limited by environment, tradition, and circumstance, he yet managed to write the finest poems written in America between 1900 and 1920. In England and Ireland were Hardy, Yeats, and Wilfrid Owen and there were Pound and Eliot to be heard. Yet if we consider calmly, apart from notions of "influence" and contemporaneity, we will be forced to admit that the latter two men's work had not by this time achieved the self-contained excellence here under discussion. For all the obvious repetitiousness and aridity of Robinson's later work, twenty years of productiveness, and productiveness of excellence, is an unusually long period for an American writer. Robinson is not Great as Dante and Shakespeare and Milton and Sophocles are Great, but he is in the very front rank of American writers.

⤇ *Selected Bibliography*

Principal Works of Edwin Arlington Robinson

The Torrent and The Night Before. Cambridge, Mass.: Privately printed, 1896.
The Children of the Night. Boston: Badger, 1897.
Captain Craig. Boston and New York: Houghton Mifflin, 1902.
The Town Down the River. New York: Scribner's, 1910.
Van Zorn. New York: Macmillan, 1914. (Play.)
The Porcupine. New York: Macmillan, 1915. (Play.)
The Man against the Sky. New York: Macmillan, 1916.
Merlin. New York: Macmillan, 1917.
Lancelot. New York: Seltzer, 1920.
The Three Taverns. New York: Macmillan, 1920.
Avon's Harvest. New York: Macmillan, 1921.
Collected Poems. New York: Macmillan, 1921.
Roman Bartholow. New York: Macmillan, 1923.
The Man Who Died Twice. New York: Macmillan, 1924.
Dionysius in Doubt. New York: Macmillan, 1925.
Tristram. New York: Macmillan, 1927.
Sonnets 1889–1927. New York: Gaige, 1928.
Cavender's House. New York: Macmillan, 1929.
Collected Poems. New York: Macmillan, 1929.
The Glory of the Nightingales. New York: Macmillan, 1930.
Selected Poems. New York: Macmillan, 1931.
Matthias at the Door. New York: Macmillan, 1931.
Nicodemus. New York: Macmillan, 1932.
Talifer. New York: Macmillan, 1933.
Amaranth. New York: Macmillan, 1934.
King Jasper. New York: Macmillan, 1935.
Collected Poems. New York: Macmillan, 1937.

Letters

Letters of Edwin Arlington Robinson to Howard George Schmitt, edited by Carl J. Weber. Waterville, Maine: Colby College Library, 1943.
Selected Letters of Edwin Arlington Robinson, with an Introduction by Ridgely Torrence. New York: Macmillan, 1940.

Selected Bibliography

Untriangulated Stars: Letters of Edwin Arlington Robinson to Harry de Forest Smith, edited by Denham Sutcliffe. Cambridge, Mass.: Harvard University Press, 1947.

Current American Reprints

Selected Early Poems and Letters of E. A. Robinson, edited by Charles T. Davis. New York: Holt, Rinehart, and Winston. $1.45.
Selected Poems of Edwin Arlington Robinson, edited by Morton D. Zabel. New York: Macmillan. $1.95.

Bibliographies

Hogan, Charles Beecher. *A Bibliography of Edwin Arlington Robinson*. New Haven: Yale University Press, 1936.
Lippincott, Lillian. *A Bibliography of the Writings and Criticism of Edwin Arlington Robinson*. Boston: Faxton, 1937.

Critical and Biographical Studies

Barnard, Ellsworth. *Edwin Arlington Robinson: A Critical Study*. New York: Macmillan, 1952.
Coffin, R. P. T. *New Poetry of New England: Frost and Robinson*. Baltimore: Johns Hopkins Press, 1938.
Fussell, Edwin S. *Edwin Arlington Robinson: The Literary Background of a Traditional Poet*. Berkeley: University of California Press, 1954.
Hagedorn, Hermann. *Edwin Arlington Robinson*. New York: Macmillan, 1938.
Kaplan, Estelle. *Philosophy in the Poetry of Edwin Arlington Robinson*. New York: Columbia University Press, 1940.
Neff, Emery. *Edwin Arlington Robinson* (American Men of Letters Series). New York: Sloane Associates, 1948.
Richards, Laura E. *E. A. R.* Cambridge, Mass.: Harvard University Press, 1936.
Winters, Yvor. *Edwin Arlington Robinson* (The Makers of Modern Literature Series). Norfolk, Conn.: New Directions, 1946.

Articles

Hudson, Hoyt H. "Robinson and Praed," *Poetry*, 61:612–20 (February 1943).
Ransom, John Crowe. "Autumn of Poetry," *Southern Review*, 1:609–23 (Winter 1936).

Scott, Winfield T. " 'The Unaccredited Profession,' " *Poetry*, 50:150–54 (June 1937).

Stevick, Robert D. "Robinson and William James," *University of Kansas City Review*, 25:293–301 (June 1959).

Tate, Allen. "Again, O Ye Laurels," *New Republic*, 76:312–13 (October 25, 1933).

Zabel, Morton D. "Robinson: The Ironic Discipline," *Nation*, 145:222–23 (August 28, 1937).

UNIVERSITY OF MINNESOTA
PAMPHLETS ON AMERICAN WRITERS

William Van O'Connor, Allen Tate, Leonard Unger, and
Robert Penn Warren, editors
Willard Thorp, Karl Shapiro, and Philip Rahv, advisers

EACH PAMPHLET, 65 CENTS

UNIVERSITY OF MINNESOTA PRESS, Minneapolis 14
Minnesota, U.S.A.